PLAYING THE

Five String Banjo

Volume 1

for Beginners Only

An introductory method for people who have never played the five string banjo before.

by Dick Weissman

edited by Dan Fox

This is the first in a series of books on the five string banjo which will cover every aspect of playing. Starting from the absolute beginning and assuming you have never played before, we will cover Seeger, Scruggs, frailing and other traditional and original styles of playing the banjo. Although no knowledge of music is necessary, we will also teach you how to read music.

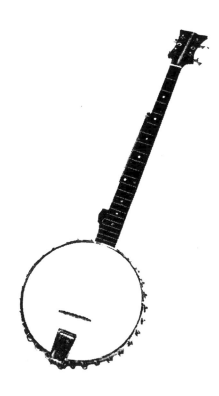

4th Edition

Copyright © 1979

The Big 3 Music Corporation
New York, N.Y.

Cover Art and Interior Design by Remo Bramanti

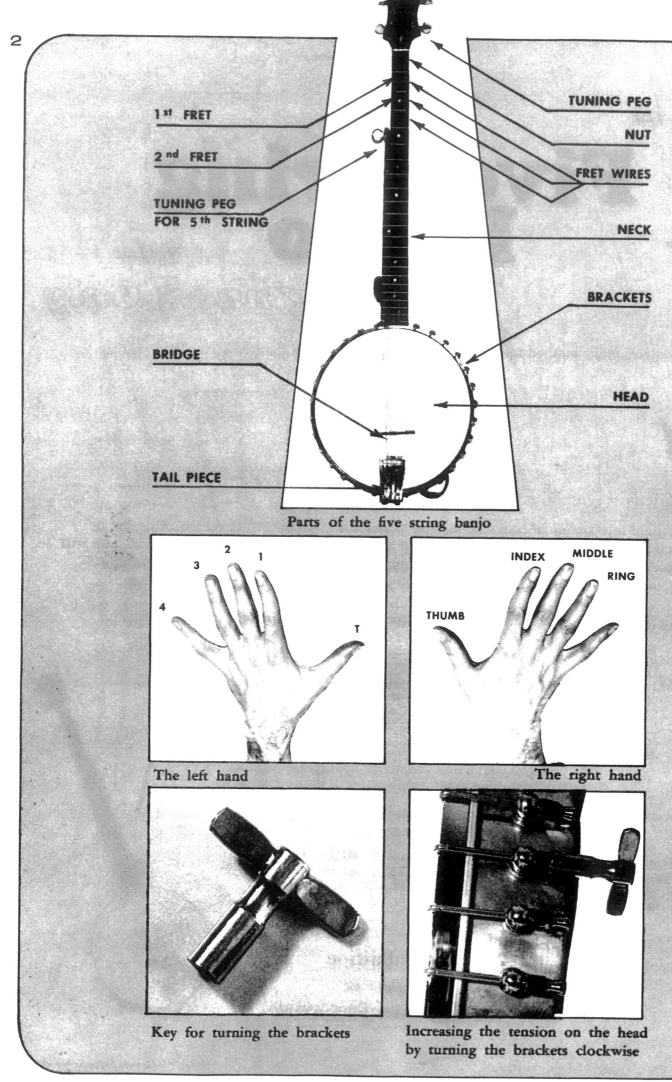

1st FRET

2nd FRET

TUNING PEG
FOR 5th STRING

TUNING PEG

NUT

FRET WIRES

NECK

BRACKETS

BRIDGE

HEAD

TAIL PIECE

Parts of the five string banjo

The left hand

The right hand

Key for turning the brackets

Increasing the tension on the head
by turning the brackets clockwise

Two ways to hold the banjo

The legs can be flat on the floor, or if you prefer to play with legs crossed, the left leg should be crossed on top of the right leg.

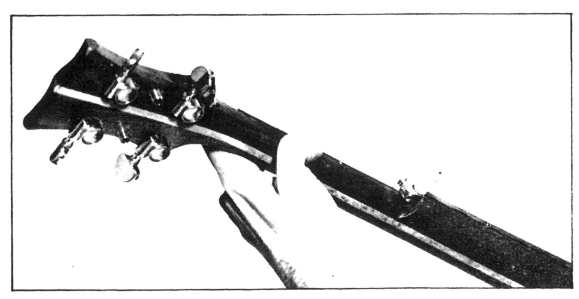

The fingers of the left hand should be arched high- the weight of the banjo is supported by the ball of the thumb. Right hand positions will be discussed later in the book according to the strum used.

When you play the banjo while standing, it is necessary to use a strap. The strap may be attached to one of the brackets of the banjo. Don't wear the banjo too low or it will be difficult to play quickly and accurately.

TUNING THE BANJO

One of the unusual characteristics of the five string banjo is that it is played in many different tunings. We will start with the G tuning which is the easiest.

Starting with the fifth (shortest) string, the strings are tuned as follows:

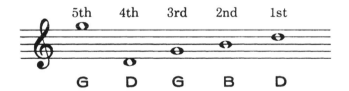

You can get the notes from a piano or from a pitch pipe. If neither of these is available you can tune in the following way:

Put your finger on the fourth string at the fifth fret and tune the open third string (without any fingers of the left hand on the frets) to it. Next place your finger on the third string at the fourth fret and tune the second string to it. When these sound the same, place your finger on the second string at the third fret and tune the first string to it. Finally place your finger on the first string at the fifth fret and tune the fifth string to it. At this point you will be in the G tuning even if the notes are not identical to the piano notes.

If you do not have a piano or pitch pipe it is advisable to check your tuning once in a while against them. If you tune the strings too low the tone will be flabby, if you tune the strings too high they may break from the extra tension.

You should change the strings every two months or so, more often if your hands sweat a lot or if you play a lot. If the tone of the strings becomes dull or the windings are wearing out it's time to change the strings. Strings come in different thicknesses (gauges) and you may want to try out different brands until you find one you prefer.

Long neck banjo

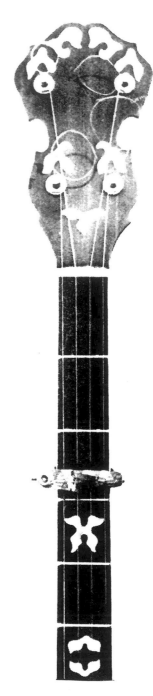

Long neck banjo with capo on 3rd fret

If you have a long neck banjo, place a capo at the third fret and tune the banjo as directed on p. 5. If you are about to buy a banjo, I recommend that you do <u>not</u> buy a long neck banjo. The advantage of having the extra three frets is offset by the clumsiness of the extra size and the difficulty of fretting the banjo in the lower positions. For reasons that are not clear to me I have always found the tone of long neck banjos to be inferior to those of normal size.

READING MUSIC FOR THE FIVE STRING BANJO

If you do not read music it is suggested that you obtain another volume in this series of books, How to Read Music for the Five String Banjo.

Below are a few rudiments of music which will provide a beginning in learning how to read. You can follow the tablature in this book, but reading notes is much quicker and has the advantage of indicating the rhythms as well as the notes. Reading also provides you with an easier means of playing with other musicians.*

	Open	1st fret	2nd fret	3rd fret	4th fret	5th fret
1st string	D	D♯	E	F	F♯	G
2nd string	B	C	C♯	D	D♯	E
3rd string	G	G♯	A	A♯	B	C
4th string	D	D♯	E	F	F♯	G
5th string	G					

The 5th string is rarely fretted.

THE STAFF AND THE NOTES

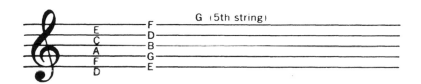

*In this book all songs have been completely written out in traditional as well as tablature notation. I suggest that the player familiarize himself with the melody by picking it out with the index finger before working on the tune. Reading tablature is easy: Below are the 1st few bars of "Skip to my Lou"

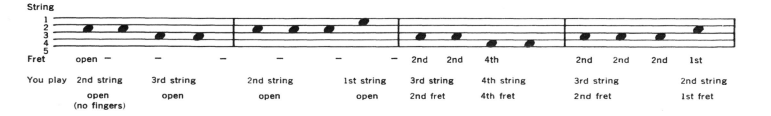

8

In order to play the first song, you will have to learn two chords, G and D7. The G chord consists simply of strumming the banjo without using the left hand at all.

Below is a diagram of the D7 chord. Place the second finger of the left hand on the third string at the 2nd fret; Place the first finger of the left hand on the second string at the 1st fret. Always finger just behind the metal bars (called fret wires). If you cross the fret wires you will get a different note.

(5th string not shown because the left hand does not finger it)

In this song you will use the middle finger of the right hand to brush down across the strings starting with the fifth string. For each beat, or quarter note, the right hand will strum one time.

Skip to my Lou

Lost my part-ner, skip to my Lou,   Lost my part-ner, skip to my Lou,

Lost my part-ner, what-'ll I do?   Skip to my Lou, my dar-lin'.

Skip to my Lou

Melody in Tablature

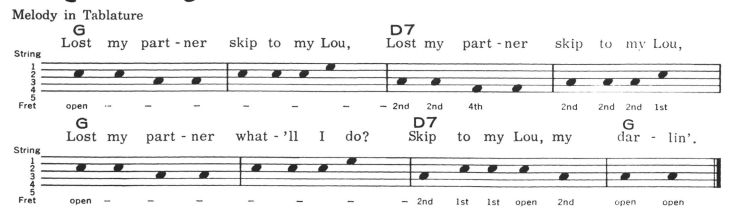

G			D7			G

Lost my part-ner skip to my Lou, Lost my part-ner skip to my Lou,

Lost my part-ner what-'ll I do? Skip to my Lou, my dar-lin'.

I'll get another one prettier than you (three times)
Skip to my Lou my darlin'.

Little red wagon painted in blue (three times)
Skip to my Lou my darlin'.

Flies in the buttermilk, shoo fly shoo (three times)
Skip to my Lou my darlin'.

Probably the hardest thing in learning the banjo at first will be having your mind and fingers memorize the chords so that they become automatic to you. After a week or so if you have practiced regularly, you should be able to play the D7 chord without looking at your left hand. Remember to keep your left hand arched, and to strum in time with the middle finger of your right hand. You might try keeping time with your foot, one foot tap for every beat.

For the song below, continue to use the same right hand pattern - one strum for each beat - four for each bar of music.

Go Tell Aunt Rhody

Go Tell Aunt Rhody

Melody in Tablature

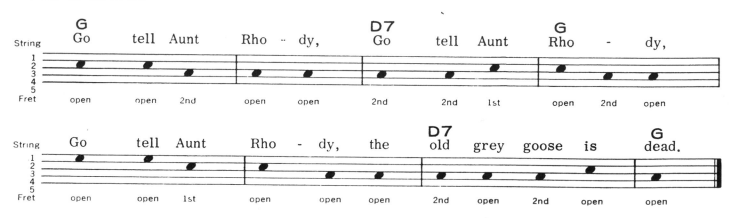

The one she's been saving (three times)
To make a feather bed.

She died in the mill pond (three times)
A standin' on her head.

The goslins are mournin' (three times)
Because their mother's dead.

BANJOVIALITIES.

(THE FREEMASONRY OF ART.)

HE. "I beg your pardon—but—er—would you be so very kind as to give me the G?"
SHE. "Oh, certainly." (*Gives it.*)
HE. "Thanks, awfully!" (*Bows, and proceeds on his way.*)

We will now change the method of right hand picking.

1. The index finger picks up (towards you) on the first, second, third or fourth string.

2. Then the middle finger brushes down across all the strings.

The rhythm is even, each step as long as the other. Do this with Polly Wolly Doodle below; Then go back and try this same strum with the songs you have already learned.

Polly Wolly Doodle

Went down south for to see my Sal, sing Pol-ly Wol-ly Doo-dle all the day, My Sal she is a pret-ty gal, sing Pol-ly Wol-ly Doo-dle all the day. Fare thee well, fare thee well, fare thee well my fair-y fay, For I'm off to Louis-i-a-na for to see my Su-sy-an-na, sing Pol-ly Wol-ly Doo-dle all the day.

* The bracket shows how long it takes to play a complete strum.

Polly Wolly Doodle

Melody in Tablature

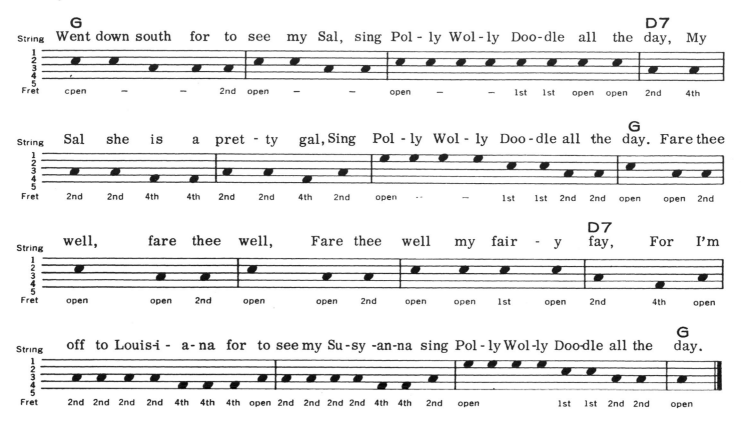

Peanut sitting on a railroad track,
Waiting for his supper
Along came a choo choo train,
Choo choo peanut butter.

Earlier songs with strum marked,

SKIP TO MY LOU

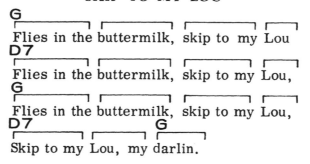

GO TELL AUNT RHODY

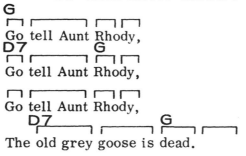

It is now time for us to learn the basic strum as used by Pete Seeger. We are going to take the strum used in the last lesson and add a step: The thumb plays the fifth string. The entire sequence looks like this:

1) Index finger picks up on 1st, 2nd, 3rd, or 4th string
   (Eventually this will be a melody note).

2) Middle finger brushes down across strings

3) Thumb plays fifth string

The rhythm is a quarter note followed by two eighth notes (♩ ♫). In other words the first note is twice as long as the other two notes in the pattern. You can say, bump dit-ty or one two-and, or whatever way you can count or tap that will help you remember.

Be sure you can play the strum evenly before you apply it to the next song,

Hush Little Baby

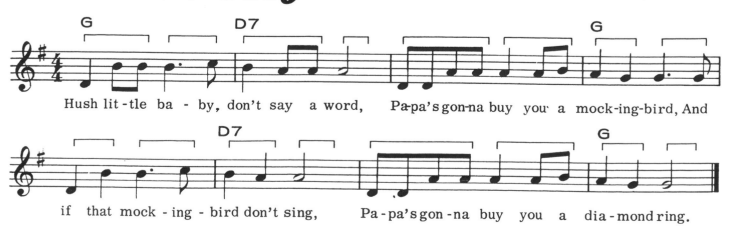

Hush lit-tle ba - by, don't say a word,   Pa-pa's gon-na buy you a mock-ing-bird, And

if that mock - ing - bird don't sing,   Pa-pa's gon-na buy you a dia-mond ring.

Hush Little Baby

Melody in Tablature

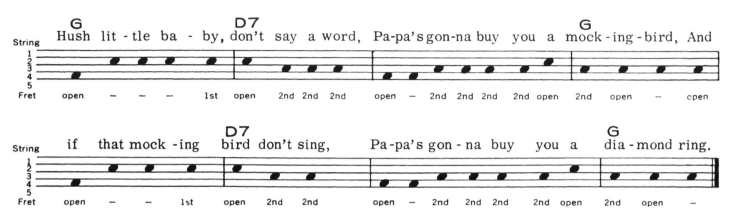

Additional Verses

And if that diamond ring is brass
Papa's gonna buy you a looking glass.

And if that looking glass gets broke
Papa's gonna buy you a billy goat.

And if that billy goat won't pull
Papa's gonna buy you a cart and bull.

And if that cart and bull turn over
Papa's gonna buy you a doggie named Rover.

And if that dog named Rover won't bark
Papa's gonna buy you a horse and cart.

And if that horse and cart fall down
You'll still be the sweetest little baby in town.

SH 4972

Here is another song to try with the basic strum. Remember to play the right rhythm; the first step of the strum is equal to the other two steps together.

Buffalo Gals

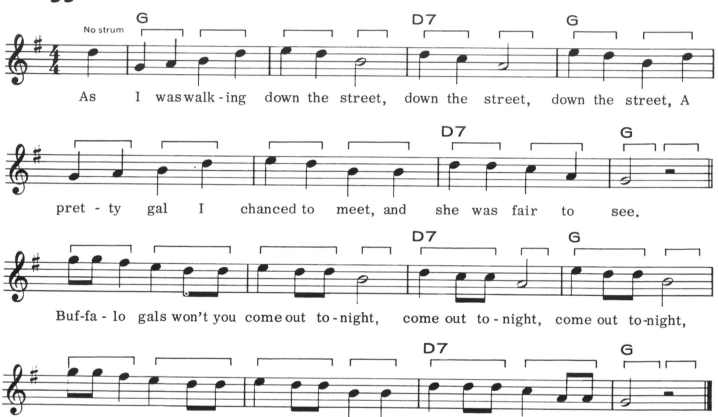

As I was walk-ing down the street, down the street, down the street, A

pret - ty gal I chanced to meet, and she was fair to see.

Buf-fa - lo gals won't you come out to-night, come out to-night, come out to-night,

Buf-fa - lo gals won't you come out to-night and dance by the light of the moon.

Buffalo Gals

Melody in Tablature

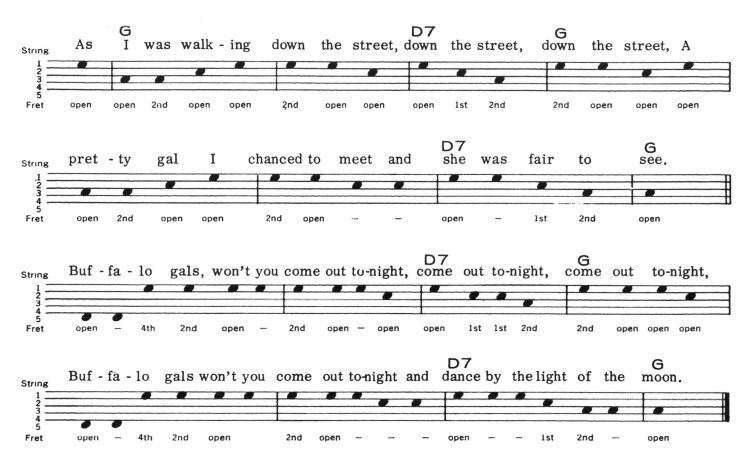

Additional Verses

I asked her if she'd marry me, marry me, marry me
I asked her if she'd marry me, and happy we could be.

We're gonna have pork and we're gonna have mutton, gonna have mutton, gonna have mutton,
If you don't come early, you won't get nothin, we'll dance by the light of the moon.

I danced with a girl with a wooden leg, wooden leg, wooden leg,
I guess that's the reason they call her Peg, and we danced by the light of the moon.

SH 4972

Here is one last song using the Basic Strum and just the two chords we have learned. By this time the chords should be automatic to you because in the next lesson we are going to learn a new chord. The song below is an old southern mountain song called WHOA MULE.

Whoa Mule

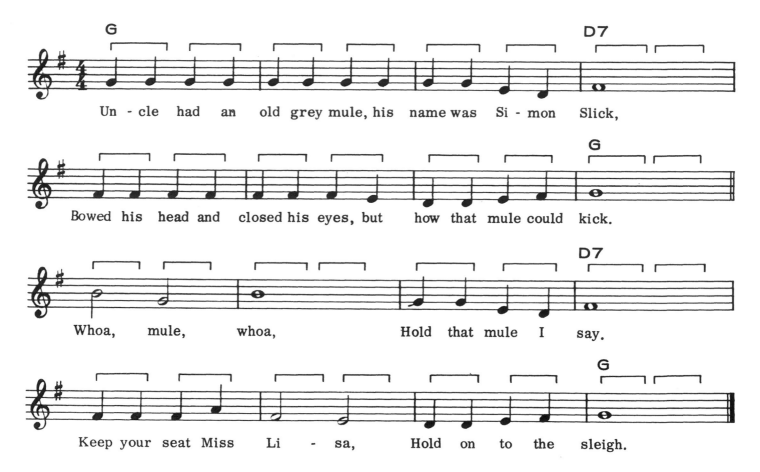

Un - cle had an old grey mule, his name was Si - mon Slick,

Bowed his head and closed his eyes, but how that mule could kick.

Whoa, mule, whoa, Hold that mule I say.

Keep your seat Miss Li - sa, Hold on to the sleigh.

Whoa Mule

Melody in Tablature

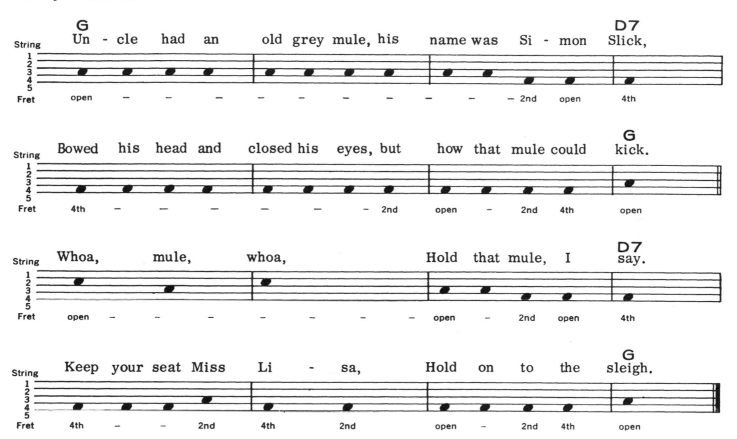

Fifteen horses in the team, the leaders they are blind,
Every time the sun goes down, pretty girls on my mind.

Went to see my gal last night she was washin' at the tub,
The more I asked her to marry me, the harder she would rub.

SH 4972

INTRODUCING THE C CHORD

It is now time to expand our repertoire of chords. The chord below is the C chord. With the G, C and D7 you will now be able to play the great majority of American folksongs. The fingering in the left hand is as follows: Finger the 1st string at the 2nd fret with the third finger of the left hand, finger the 2nd string at the first fret with the first finger of the left hand and finger the 4th string at the 2nd fret with the second finger of the left hand. You must keep the left hand arched or the 2nd finger will probably slide onto the third string and produce a blurred sound. All of the notes should be clear. Below is the chord diagram.

You are now ready to play your first three-chord song:

Red River Valley

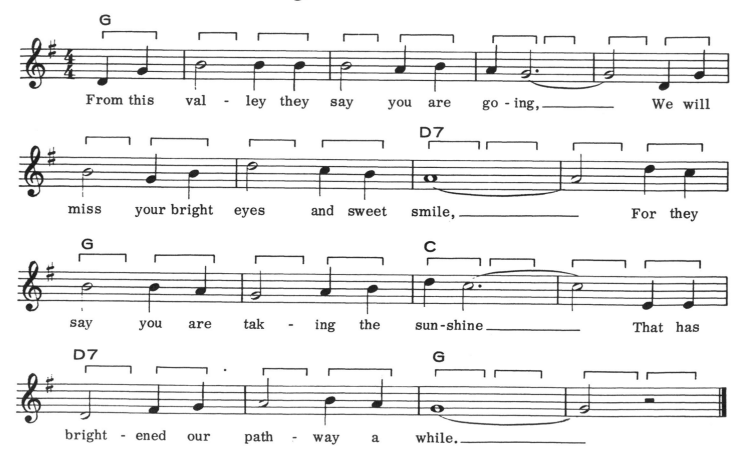

Red River Valley

Melody in Tablature

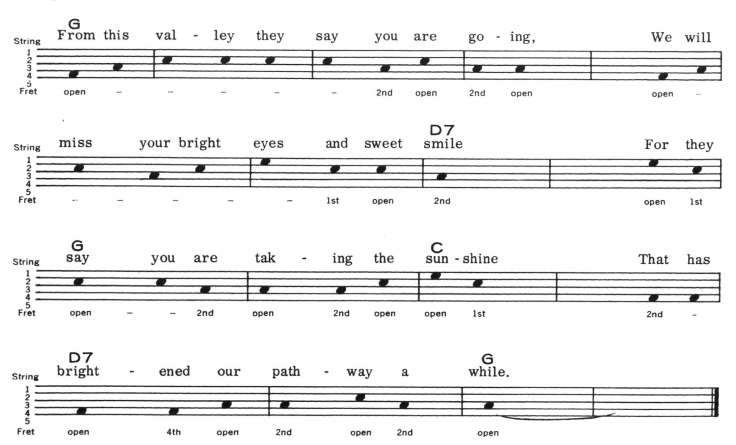

Come and sit by my side if you love me
Do not hasten to bid me adieu
But remember the Red River Valley
And that girl who has loved you so true.

From this valley they say you are going
When you go, may your darling go too?
Would you leave her behind, unprotected
When she loves no other but you.

As you go to your home by the ocean
May you never forget those sweet hours
That we spent in the Red River Valley
And the love we exchanged 'mid the flowers

Below is another song using the G, C and D7 chords and the basic strum. By this time you should be getting used to the C chord. Remember to practice slowly, the faster you play the faster you will have to make the chord changes.

Oh Susanna

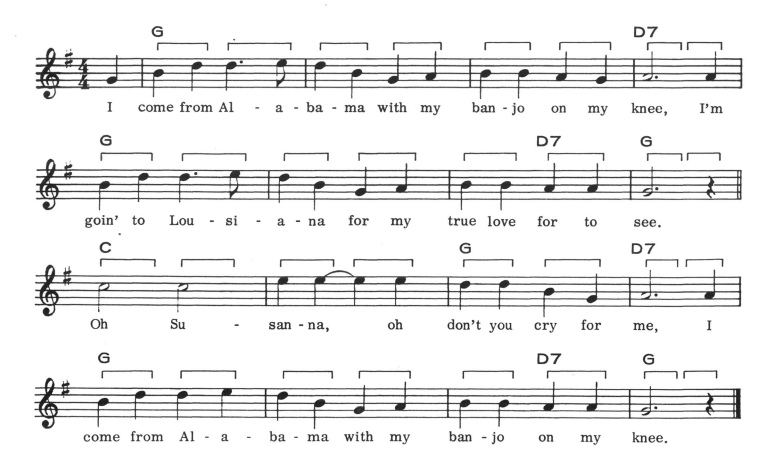

I come from Al - a - ba - ma with my ban - jo on my knee, I'm goin' to Lou - si - a - na for my true love for to see. Oh Su - san - na, oh don't you cry for me, I come from Al - a - ba - ma with my ban - jo on my knee.

Oh Susanna

Melody in Tablature

Additional Verses

It rained all night the day I left
The weather it was dry
The sun so hot I froze to death
Susanna don't you cry.

I had a dream the other night
When everything was still
I dreamt I saw Susanna dear
A-coming down the hill.

SH 4972

HAMMERING ON

It is possible to play notes with the left hand on the banjo without using the right hand at all! This technique is called *hammering on.*

It can be done in two ways:

Finger a D7 chord. Lift your left hand off the third string at the second fret. With the right index finger, pick the third string open.

Then come down on the third string at the second fret with the second finger of the left hand.

(The second way of hammering on is discussed on page 26.)

When playing LONDON BRIDGE you may hammer on either of the fingered notes in the D7 chord by lifting one finger of the left hand off the fret as described above.

The complete Basic Strum with hammering on breaks down as follows:
1) Lift one finger of left hand off a chord while the right index finger picks up on that string.
2) Hammer down on the string you just picked with the normal left hand finger (as described above).
3) Middle finger brushes down across strings.
4) Thumb plays fifth string.

The rhythm of the strum will now be four even eighth notes (♪ ♪ ♪ ♪).

The complete strum pattern is represented on the arrangement by a bracket ⌐¬.

London Bridge

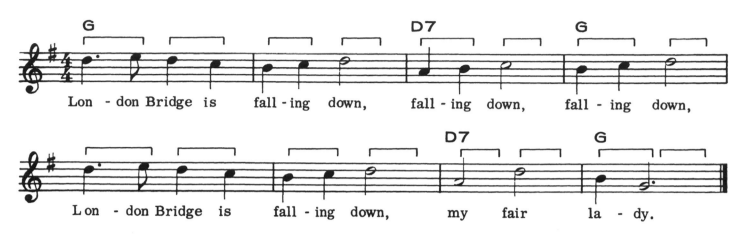

Lon - don Bridge is fall - ing down, fall - ing down, fall - ing down,

Lon - don Bridge is fall - ing down, my fair la - dy.

London Bridge

Melody in Tablature

Additional Verses

Pick it up if it falls down,
It falls down, it falls down,
Pick it up if it falls down
My fair lady.

Build it up with sticks and stones,
Sticks and stones, sticks and stones,
Build it up with sticks and stones
My fair lady.

SH 4972

MORE ON HAMMERING ON

Now try hammering on with the C chord. Again you may use any of the notes that are fingered in the left hand to hammer on. Try it with the Crawdad Song.

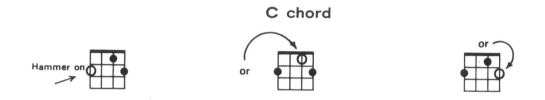

C chord

Crawdad Song

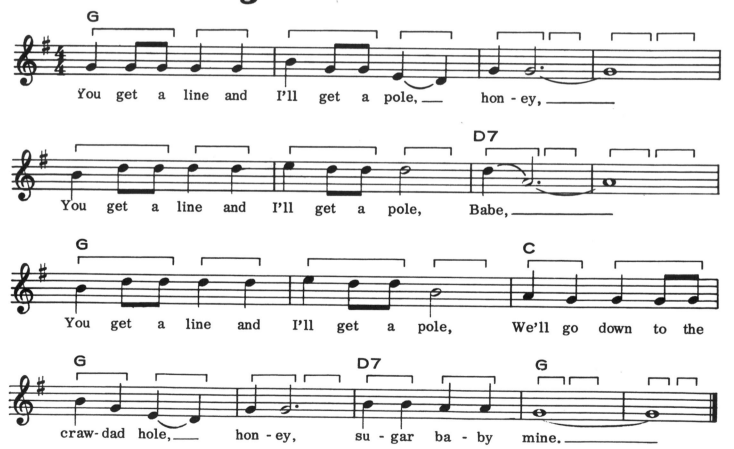

Crawdad Song

Melody in Tablature

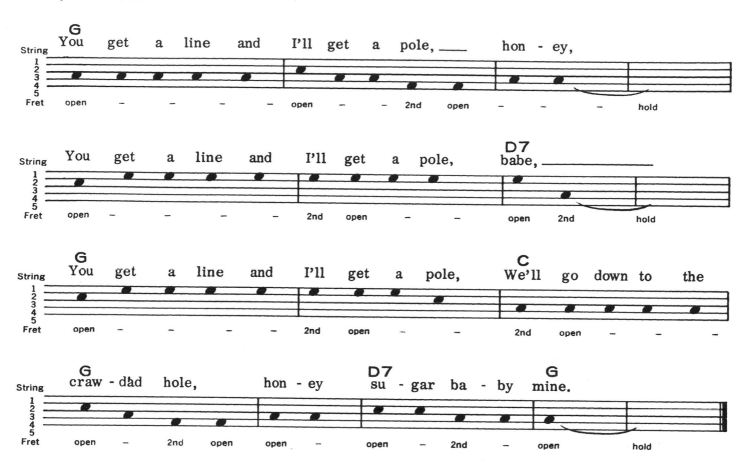

Hurry up babe you slept too late, baby,
Hurry up babe you slept too late, babe,
Hurry up babe you slept too late,
Crawdad man done passed your gate,
Honey, sugar baby mine.

Sell your crawdads three for a dime, honey
Sell your crawdads three for a dime, babe
Sell your crawdads three for a dime
Your crawdads ain't good as mine,
Honey, sugar baby mine.

SH 4972

HAMMERING ON THE G CHORD

You have now used hammering on with the C and D7 chords. It is also possible to hammer on with the G chord. Play the G chord then hammer on the 4th string at the 2nd fret. Although this note is not in the chord itself it is a pleasant ornament. You may also hammer on the 3rd string at the 2nd fret when playing the G chord. (See diagram below.)

ADVANCED HAMMERING ON

Now you have seen that it is possible to hammer on notes not in the chord itself. It is also possible to hammer on in the left hand on one string while picking another string with the right hand. Try playing a G chord; with the index finger of the right hand play the first string, then hammer on with the 2nd finger of the left hand on the 4th string at the 2nd fret. In many ways this is a more effective way of hammering on because the difference in pitch and tone quality between the note picked and the note hammered on makes it sound almost as though two banjos are playing! In the diagrams below I have suggested some notes to hammer on not in the G, C or D7 chords. Try these picking a different string than the one you are hammering on. To correctly execute advanced hammering on it is crucial for your left hand attacks on the hammered notes to be quick and decisive.

ADDITIONAL NOTES FOR HAMMERING ON

G chord
(see above)

C chord

Don't finger 4th string with this. Then alternate hammering on 4th string 2nd fret with 3rd string 2nd fret.

D7 chord

Don't finger 3rd string with this. Then alternate hammering on 4th string 2nd fret with 3rd string 2nd fret.

Sourwood Mountain

Chick-en's crow-in' on Sour-wood Moun-tain, Hey ding dum did-dle um day.

So man-y pret-ty girls I can't count them, Hey ding dum did-dle-um day.

Sourwood Mountain

Melody in Tablature

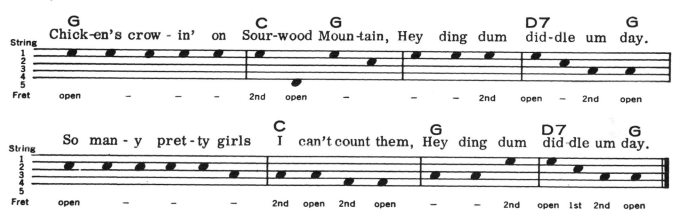

Additional Verses

My true love lives up the holler,
Hey, ding dum, diddle um day,
She won't come and I won't call her,
Hey ding dum diddle um day.

My true love's a blue eyed daisy,
Hey, ding dum diddle um day
If she don't come I'll soon go crazy,
Hey ding dum diddle um day.

For our last selection with hammering on, try Jesse James. By this time you should be able to hammer on freely with a very smooth sound.

Jesse James

Jesse James

Melody in Tablature

Additional Verses

It was Robert Ford, that dirty little coward
I wonder how he does feel
He ate of Jesse's bread, and he slept in Jesse's bed
And he laid poor Jesse in his grave

It was on a Saturday night, Jesse was at home
Talking with his family brave;
Robert Ford came along, like a thief in the night
And laid poor Jesse in his grave

3/4 TIME

So far we have only dealt with songs in 4/4 time. You have probably already tried to play some songs in 3/4 or waltz time, such as Down In The Valley, On Top of Old Smoky, etc., and found yourself unable to do so, A simple modification of the basic strum makes it possible to play in 3/4 time. This goes as follows:

1) Index finger of the right hand picks up on any single string
2) Either hammer on one of the strings or simply hold the first note as in the regular basic strum
3) Middle finger of right hand brushes down across strings
4) Thumb plays fifth string
5) Middle finger of the right hand brushes down across strings
6) Thumb plays fifth string

In other words you simply repeat steps 3 and 4. The rhythm is six even eighth notes. (♩♩♩♩♩♩), or, if step 2 is held rather than hammered, (♩ ♩♩♩♩).

Below is our first song in 3/4 time:

Down in the Valley

Down in the Valley

Melody in Tablature

Roses love sunshine, violets love dew
Angels in heaven know I love you
Know I love you dear, know I love you
Angels in heaven know I love you

Write me a letter, send it by mail
Send it in care of Birmingham jail
Birmingham jail, love, Birmingham jail
Send it in care of Birmingham jail

SH 4972

ANOTHER SONG IN 3/4 TIME

When playing in 3/4 time there should be a strong accent on the first beat (step one of our strum). Most songs in 3/4 tend to be smooth and should not be played rapidly, so here is another chance to practice your strumming so it becomes smooth and consistent. Below is the famous folk song On Top of Old Smoky. Use the same strum as in Down In the Valley.

On Top of Old Smoky

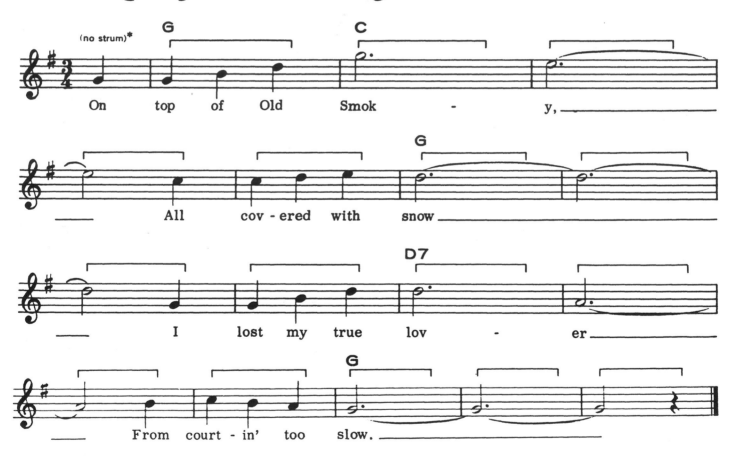

* Instead of omitting the strum here, you may give an extra up-pick or a brush stroke followed by the thumb.

On Top of Old Smoky

Melody in Tablature

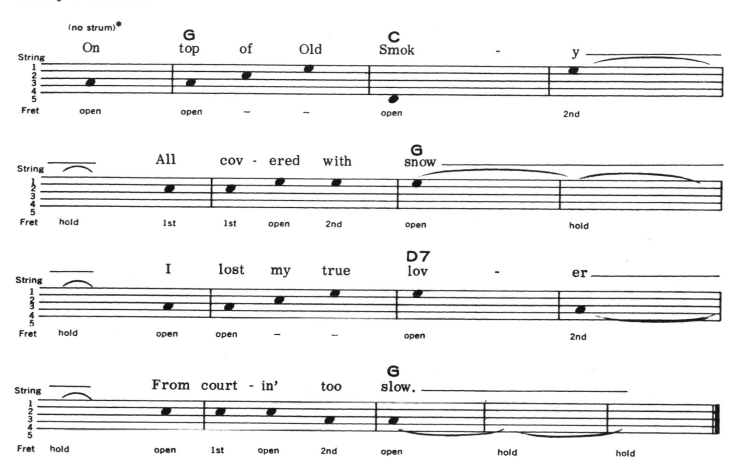

For courting's a pleasure but parting is grief
And a false hearted lover is worse than a thief

For a thief he will rob you and take all you have
But a false hearted lover will lead you to the grave

And the grave will decay you and turn you to dust
Not one girl in twenty that a poor boy can trust

* Instead of omitting the strum here, you may give an extra up-pick or a brush stroke followed by the thumb.

SH 4972

THE C TUNING

There are a number of different tunings used in playing the five string banjo. The one that we have played in is the G tuning. We are now going to learn the C tuning. Tune the 4th string down a whole tone, from D to C. In playing the banjo in this tuning the 4th string at the 7th fret sounds the same as the 3rd open string. You will remember that in the G tuning the 4th string at the 5th fret sounded the same as the 3rd string open.

First of all here are two chords in the C tuning, C and G7. Try the old song, Merrily We Roll Along using the basic strum.

Merrily We Roll Along

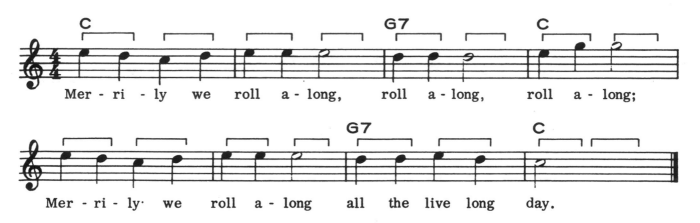

Mer - ri - ly we roll a - long, roll a - long, roll a - long;

Mer - ri - ly· we roll a - long all the live long day.

Merrily We Roll Along

Melody in Tablature

HERE IS ANOTHER SONG IN 3/4 OR WALTZ TIME USING THE C TUNING.

Use the basic strum with this song as indicated below:
1 Index finger of the right hand picks up on any single string
2 Middle finger of the right hand brushes down across strings
3 Thumb plays fifth string
4 Middle finger of right hand brushes down across strings
5 Thumb plays fifth string
The rhythm is one quarter note and four even eighth notes (♩ ♫♫).

Clementine

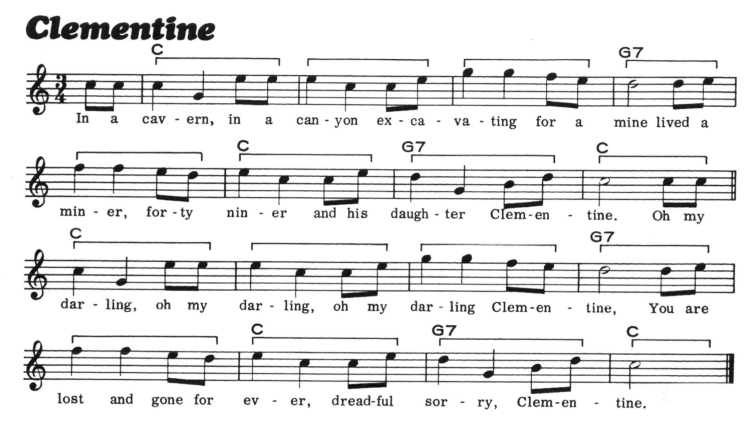

Clementine

Melody in Tablature

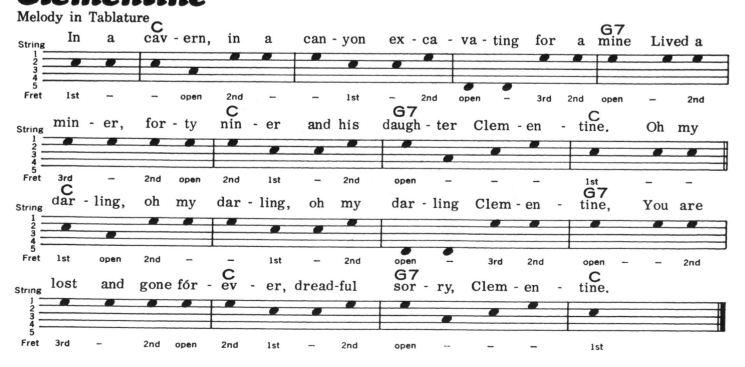

MORE ON THE C TUNING

The F chord in the C tuning

F chord

Three Basic Chords in the C tuning with notes to be hammered on indicated by a O

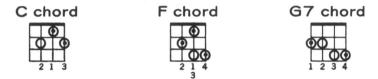

At this point you should be very familiar with the technique of hammering on. The best way to use this technique is not to do an entire song with it, but to do one verse with hammering on followed by one without it. Or you may alternate hammering on with the simple basic strum: first one, then another within one verse. This is very important because either technique can become dull with too much repetition.

Next we have the famous country song Wabash Cannonball. It is played in the C tuning using the C, F, and G7 chords.

SH 4972

Wabash Cannonball

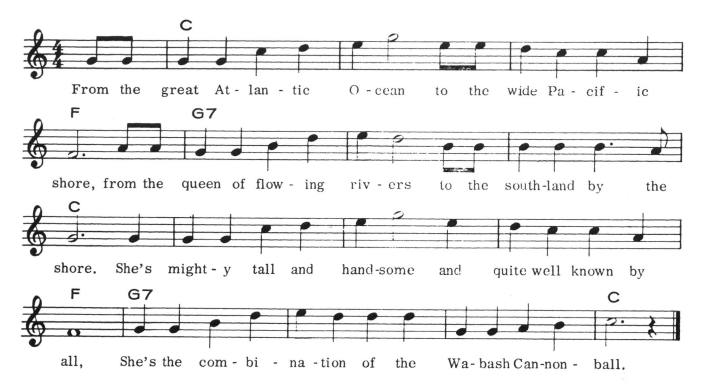

From the great At - lan - tic O - cean to the wide Pa - cif - ic shore, from the queen of flow - ing riv - ers to the south-land by the shore. She's might - y tall and hand-some and quite well known by all, She's the com - bi - na - tion of the Wa-bash Can-non - ball.

Wabash Cannonball

Melody in Tablature

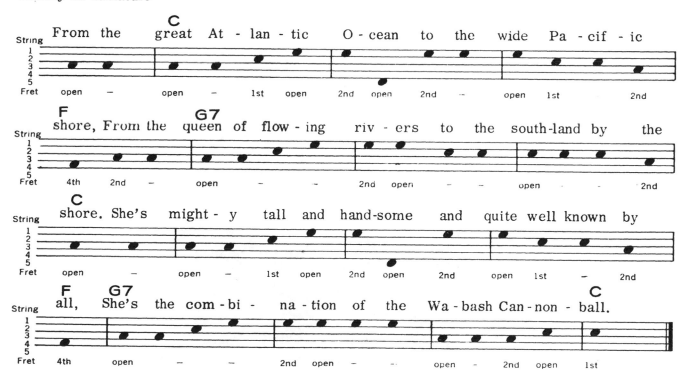

From the great At - lan - tic O - cean to the wide Pa - cif - ic shore, From the queen of flow - ing riv - ers to the south-land by the shore. She's might - y tall and hand-some and quite well known by all, She's the com - bi - na - tion of the Wa - bash Can - non - ball.

Listen to the jingle, the rumble and the roar
As she glides along the woodland, through the hills and by the shore,

Hear the mighty rush of the engine, the lonesome hobo's squall,
Travelling through the jungles on the Wabash Cannonball.

PULLING OFF

A technique often used in conjunction with hammering on, although not quite as useful, is called pulling off. In pulling off the left hand actually picks a note as though it were the picking hand. With a C chord in the C tuning the sequence is as follows:

1) Index finger picks up on any single string.
2) Second finger of the left hand pulls off first string at 2nd fret.
3) Middle finger of right hand brushes down across strings.
4) Thumb plays fifth string.

The rhythm again is four even eighth notes ().

Be careful not to pull the string too hard or you will pull it off the fingerboard and get an unpleasant sound.

Try the old favorite Careless Love, pulling off with the C chord as described above.

C chord

← note to be pulled off

Careless Love

Love, oh love oh care-less love, Love, oh love oh care-less love,

Love, oh love, oh care-less love, oh see what love has done to me.

Careless Love

Melody in Tablature

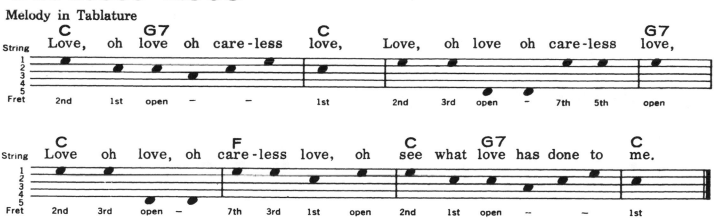

Sorrow, sorrow to my heart (3 times)
Since me and my true love had to part

Once I wore my apron low (3 times)
Could hardly keep you from my door

Now my apron strings won't pin (3 times)
You pass my door and you won't come in.

SH 4972

PULLING OFF, CONTINUED

As in the case of hammering on, pulling off may be done with any chord. Below are diagrams of where to pull off with the C, F or G7 chords.

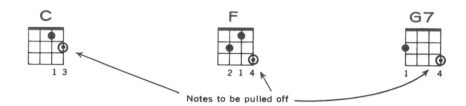

Again as in hammering on, you can pull off one string while picking another. Also remember that this technique can become tiresome with too much repetition. It also can be alternated with hammering on or the simple basic strum. A typical song accompaniment might be: Verse 1-Basic Strum; Verse 2-Basic Strum and Hammering On; Verse 3-Basic Strum with Pulling Off, etc. Or, pulling off can be used between verses as a vamp while waiting to start the next verse. This is adviseable, because you seldom sing a song without some kind of pause between the verses.

* * * * *

Try Worried Man Blues, pulling off with all of the chords as diagrammed above. Please note that the most practical notes to pull off are on the first string because they are the easiest to control with the left hand.

Worried Man Blues

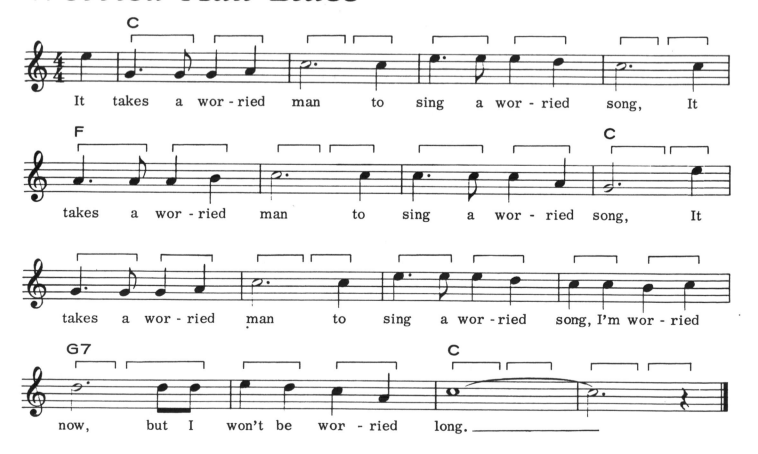

Worried Man Blues

Melody in Tablature

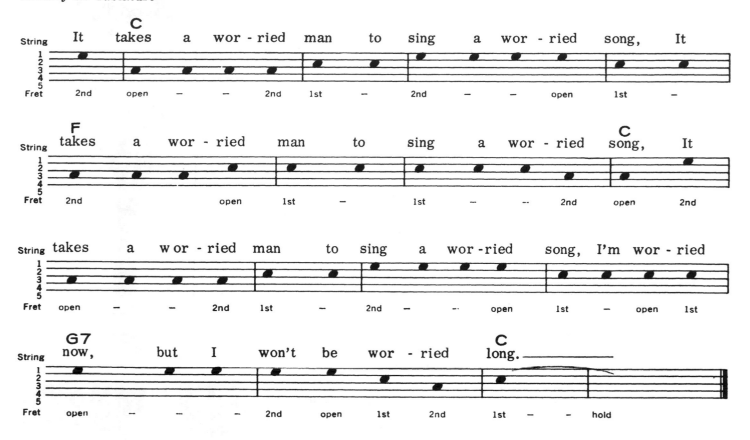

I went across the river, and I lay down to sleep (3 times)
When I woke up I had shackles on my feet.

I went up to the judge, said what's going to be my fine (3 times)
He said twenty years, on the Rocky Mountain line.

PULLING OFF IN THE G TUNING

Below are diagrams of notes that can be pulled off in the G tuning with the three chords we've covered. Go back to some of the songs you've learned and try these. It is not recommended to pull off in songs in 3/4 time because the rough sound of the notes interferes with the flow of the song.

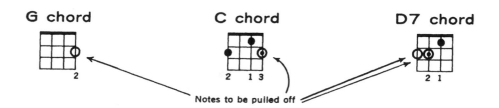

Sometimes you will be playing a song, say in the key of C, and find that key too low in pitch for you to sing comfortably. By using the capo you may change the key to a higher pitch without changing the fingerings of the chords.

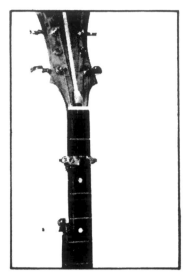

In the C tuning the capo at the 2nd fret will give you the key of D. You must finger as though the capo indicated the beginning of the banjo neck.

You must, however, retune the 5th string when using the capo. To retune the fifth string to any pitch above A, it is necessary to put a screw in the fingerboard five frets above the fifth string peg itself. When retuning with the capo, you slip the fifth string under the screw and then tune it. Pete Seeger recommends leaving 1/32" clearance under the head of the screw so you can slip the string under it. (See his book How To Play The Five String Banjo, an interesting book for more advanced players.)

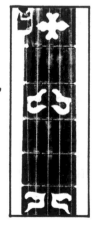
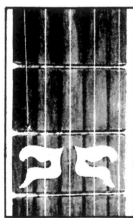

Below is a chart which tells you what key the capo puts you in at different frets in the C and G tunings.

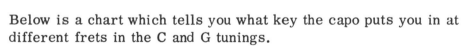

	C tuning	G tuning
Capo at 1st fret	C♯	G♯
Capo at 2nd fret	D	A
Capo at 3rd fret	D♯	A♯
Capo at 4th fret	E	B
Capo at 5th fret	F	C
Capo at 6th fret	F♯	C♯

Note: If you have the long-necked or Seeger model banjo, the tuning open is A in C tuning or E in G tuning, at the first fret this will become A♯ or F, at the second fret B or F♯, and at the third fret fret C or G, as with the normal five string banjo.

BUYING A BANJO

When you first buy a banjo you will probably not want to spend too much money. Sometimes you can find a good banjo second hand in a pawn shop, music store, second hand store or through newspaper advertisements. About the best cheap banjo that I have run across new is the Iida, made in Japan, which sells for less than $150. Morris makes a comparable model, and the Raimi, which is made in Seattle, sells for under $250. In the better quality banjos the best makers are Gibson, Ode, Ome, Stelling and Vega.

If you want to play only bluegrass music, the Gibson Mastertone and Stelling banjos are about the best made, but they sell for around $1000. A reasonable compromise is the Alvarez, Aria and Ibanez banjos which sell for around $400-500, and are basically imitations of the Gibson. The Eagle Banjo Co. of Athens, Ohio makes an excellent banjo kit for about $150-250, depending on the model you buy. You need to finish the necks and assemble the parts in these kits, so you may want to find someone who has put one together before you get involved. This edition of the book is being compiled in summer 1979, so prices may be higher when you read the book.

If you are buying a used banjo try to see if the neck is straight. Best of all go to the store with someone who has some playing experience and have him play the banjo in the higher fingerings to check its tone and accuracy. The Martin guitar company has taken over Vega and may start to make some of the older Vega models again. They were fine quality banjos. If you're looking for old banjos other makes of good quality were Bacon, Stewart, Washburn (rare), Fairbanks and Weymann.

Even high priced or recommended models may vary according to the quality of the individual instrument, as a car or any other tool or appliance may; so if you can do so, select your instrument with the aid of an experienced player or your teacher.

SPECIAL NOTE

It is important that your bridge be in the right place for the banjo to play in tune on the higher frets. The distance from the nut of the banjo to the twelfth fret should be equal to the distance from the twelfth fret to the bridge.

SELECTING A TEACHER, ETC.

If you are able to afford it, it is of great value to find a private instructor. Try to make sure that he really does play the instrument, and will not simply teach you strumming with a pick as in the tenor banjo. In many cities there are shops that specialize in folk music sales or repair, sometimes they give lessons themselves, or they will usually be able to recommend a reputable teacher. Below is a brief and incomplete list of such shops, which also generally can do repair work on banjos.

Arkansas	Erickson's String Clinic, Eureka Springs, Ark.
California	Jon Lundberg's 2126 Dwight Way Berkeley,Calif.
	Mc Cabe's 3103 W. Pico Los Angeles, Calif.
	Satterlee & Chapin 391 Ellis St. San Francisco, Calif.
	Erika Banjos 14731 Lull St. Van Nuys, Calif.
Colorado	The Music Store, 2045 Broadway, Boulder, Colo.
	Denver Folklore Center 708 E. 17th Ave. Denver, Colo.
Illinois	Fret Shop 5210 S. Harper Ave. Chicago, Ill.
	Old Town Folklore Center 911 W. Armitage Chicago, Ill.
Maryland	Gotzmer String Instruments 7900 Shirley Court,Clinton, Md.
Massachusetts	Wurlitzer 76 Bedford St. Boston, Mass.
Michigan	Ann Arbor Folklore Center 516 E. Williams St. Ann Arbor
	Elderly Instruments 541 E. Grand River Lansing, Mich.
Minnesota	Here Inc. 410 Cedar Ave. Minneapolis, Minn.
Montana	Bitterroot Music 200 S. 3rd St. W., Missoula, Montana
New Mexico	The Candyman 135 E.Water St., Santa Fe, New Mexico
New York	Folklore Center 321 6th Ave. N.Y.,N.Y.
	Matt Umanov 35 Bedford St. N.Y.,N.Y.
Oregon	Banjo & Fiddle Shop 6229 SE Milwaukee Ave. Portland, Ore.
Pennsylvania	Bucks County Folk Shop 40 Sand Road, New Britain, Penna.
	The Music Emporium 5437 Walnut St. Pittsburgh, Penna.
South Dakota	Shrine of Music 2035 Vermilion St. Vermilion, S.D.
Tennessee	GTR 111 4th Ave. N.Nashville, Tenn.
Virginia	Vintage Music Co. 1137 N. Highland St. Arlington, Va.
Washington, D.C.	The Guitar Shop 1860 M St.NW Wash. D.C.
Wisconsin	Folklore Center 1021 Milwaukee St. Kewaunee, Wisc.
Canada	Country Music Sales, Lantz, Nova Scotia
	Toronto Folklore Center, Toronto, Ontario

For a more complete listing of folk shops see The Folk Music Sourcebook, by Larry Sandberg and Dick Weissman, published by Alfred Knopf.

TRANSPOSITION

In many song books you will see songs written out in other keys than C or G. Below is a chart that will enable you to transpose songs from one key to another.

Key or Note	I					IV		V				
C	C	C#	D	D#	E	F	F#	G	G#	A	A#	B
C#	C#	D	D#	E	F	F#	G	G#	A	A#	B	C
D	D	D#	E	F	F#	G	G#	A	A#	B	C	C#
D#	D#	E	F	F#	G	G#	A	A#	B	C	C#	D
E	E	F	F#	G	G#	A	A#	B	C	C#	D	D#
F	F	F#	G	G#	A	A#	B	C	C#	D	D#	E
F#	F#	G	G#	A	A#	B	C	C#	D	D#	E	F
G	G	G#	A	A#	B	C	C#	D	D#	E	F	F#
G#	G#	A	A#	B	C	C#	D	D#	E	F	F#	G
A	A	A#	B	C	C#	D	D#	E	F	F#	G	G#
A#	A#	B	C	C#	D	D#	E	F	F#	G	G#	A
B	B	C	C#	D	D#	E	F	F#	G	G#	A	A#

Most common chords

Banjo Key → C

Banjo Key → G

Please note that Db = C#, Eb = D#, Gb = F#, Ab = G#, Bb = A#

USING THE TRANSPOSITION CHART

Let's say you are trying to play a piece in the key of F. You look through the song and find it contains the F, Bb and C7 chords. The closest five string banjo key is G. Since G is two steps below F on the chart, find the three chords on the F line and move each one down two steps. This will give you the chords G, C and D7, all chords which you can play.

If transposing the song to the key of G makes it too high you can transpose it to the other banjo key, the key of C. Since C is five steps above F, simply move each chord on the F line up five steps. This will give you the chords C, F and G7, also familiar to you. In a similar manner any key may be transposed to the keys of C or G.

TRANSPOSING MELODY NOTES

The same method can be used to transpose melody notes. Suppose you find an arrangement of a song in the key of Ab (G#). The first three notes of the melody are Eb (D#), Ab (G#) and Bb (A#). In order to transpose these to the key of C, find the names of the notes on the Ab (G#) line and move each one up eight steps (C is eight steps above Ab (G#)). These notes would then become G, C and D. If you wanted to play the same three notes in the key of G, they would become D, G and A (up 1 step).

48

Below are chord diagrams for common chords in the G and C tunings.

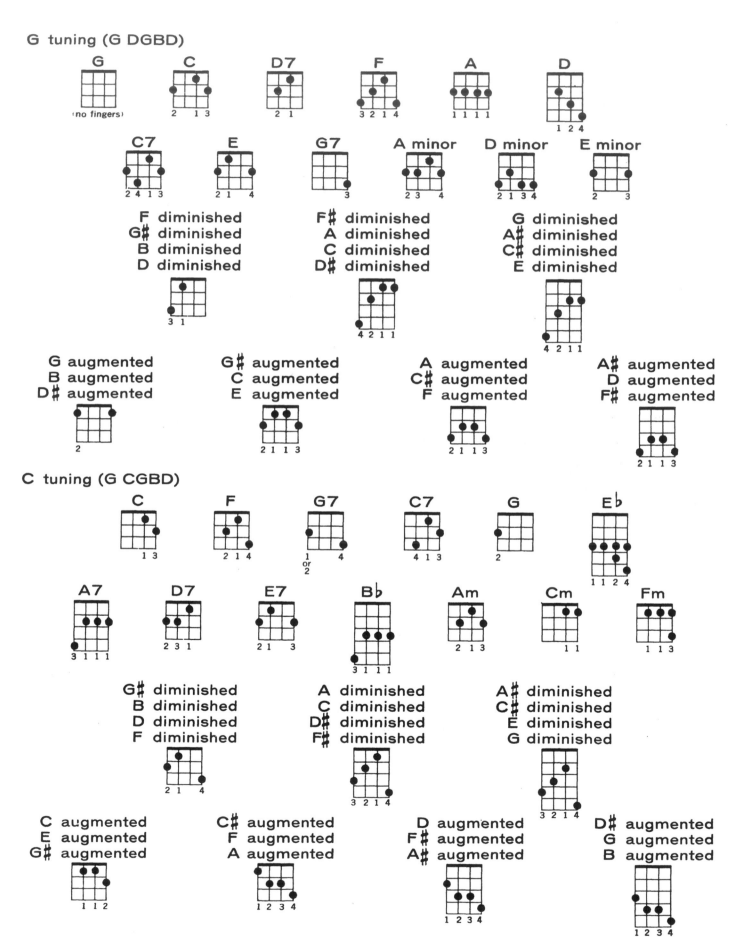